Pressure Cooker
Ultimate Pressure Cooker Recipes
(For Those Who Like Pressure Cooking)

Clark Peterson

TERMS & CONDITIONS

No part of this physical book can be transmitted or reproduced in any form, including photocopying, electronic, print, scanning, recording or mechanical without prior written permission of the author. All information, ideas & guidelines are for educational purpose only. Though the author has tried to ensure the utmost accuracy of content, all readers are advised to follow instructions at their risk. The author of this book cannot be held liable for any incidental damage, personal or commercial caused by misrepresentation of information. Readers are encouraged to seek professional help when needed.

TABLE OF CONTENTS

Chapter 1 – Pressure Cooker Recipes.. 1

Stunning Beef cooker tacos....... 2

Duke Butternut Squash Soup 6

Yummy Chinese Spare Ribs with Garlic 10

Fantasy APPLESAUCE 14

King sized Apple Cider Breakfast Pulled Beef.............. 17

Speedy Chicken foresaw 19

Epic Lentil Breakfast Risotto .. 22

Delicious Pork Chops and Cabbage in Mushroom Sauce.. 25

Mystical CARROT CAKE OATS.. 29

Super Breakfast Red Beans with Sausages 32

Supreme Garlic Bread 34

Legendary Oatmeal with Caramelized apples 37

Extraordinary Cook BAKED BANANAS 41

Awesome Crustless Bacon Quiche 44

Fantasy Lamb roasts with herb sauce 47

Mystical EINKORN & YOGURT 51

Awesome Ham Egg Muffins ... 54

Fantastic Pressure cooker fruity beef stew 57

Legendary ITALIAN OMELETTE 60

Forgotten LADI PAV 64

Lovely Mediterranean Artichoke Breakfast Casserole 68

Amazing Sweet Meatloaf 71

Mega MEXICAN BREAKFAST BURRITO 74

Tasty Soy Bean Chickpea Paste 77

Fast OUEF EN COCOTTE 79

King-sized Sweet Potato Bread Pudding 82

Cute POTATO BACON HASH BROWN 85

Historic SAUSAGE, PEPPERS, and ONIONS 88

Chapter 1 – Pressure Cooker Recipes

Discover these amazingly quick & easy pressure cooker recipes!

This book contains the amazing & best pressure cooker recipes in the world. The question is will you choose to learn this amazing method of cooking the right way or will you continue to make the same, boring recipes? Your choice

Stunning Beef cooker tacos

You know, I used to go to neighbour's house to eat this One. I used to stand in the kitchen, while my amazing cook used to prepare this recipe. I once saw him making this recipe & I knew how he made it.

Ingredients:

- Black pepper 2 - 3 tips
- One-two onions
- Garlic powder One-two tsp
- Lemon juice 2 - 3 tbsps
- Vinegar, three tablespoons
- Green chilies, two-four shredded
- 2-3 tablespoons of olive oil
- Beef broth, 1/2 half cup
- Garlic cloves

- Ground beef mince, half pound One/Two
- Garlic and ginger paste 2 - 3 tbsp
- 2 Tomatoes
- Salt as required

Method:

1. Assemble all the ingredients at one place.
2. In a separate bowl, add ground beef mince to it.
3. Combine the dried what you need to the mince and mix well till all ingredients are entirely mixed.
4. Please combine the remaining ingredients to the mixture and mix well.

5. Now we can proceed to the succeeding most important step.
6. Shift all ingredients to the pressure cooker and add broth to it as well.
7. Now you should add tsp of oil to it if you want.
8. Cover the cooker & switch the stove on for about eighteen minutes.
9. Release the pressure by lifting the weights afterwards switching the stove off.
10. One thing remains to be done now.
11. Do not open the cover until all pressure gets released.

12.   Take out the cooked meal and now you can serve.
13.   Smell the aroma and now serve.

I saw the recipe on a tv show; I instantly learnt it by heart. Ever wondered what makes the cooks now prepare such delicious food? Well, the answer is the excellent recipe they employ...

Duke Butternut Squash Soup

Soups can be very refreshing!!

Ingredients

- 1/3 cup old-fashiOned oats
- Two large celery ribs, cut 2-inch pieces
- 1/2 teaspoon salt, to taste
- About 1/4 cup of snipped fresh chives or maybe 1/4 cup thinly sliced scallion sprinkle, garnish
- 3 cups water, see note
- 1-2 lbs butternut squash,
- About 1 1/2 tablespoons of instant vegetable stock powder
- 2 - 3 tablespoons water
- Two-three tsp herbs de Provence

- One 1/2 cups thinly sliced leeks or maybe 1 1/2 cups coarsely shredded onions
- 2-3 tsp sherry wine vinegar or maybe 2 - 3 tsp balsamic vinegar

the method of preparation

1. Assemble all the ingredients at one place.
2. Finely chop squash.
3. A food processor works well here. You should have five cups.
4. Finely chop celery. Set apart with squash.
5. Now we may proceed to the next most important step. Heat Two tablespoons of

water and saute the leeks for 1 minute.
6. Saute the leeks for 1 minute.
7. Now you should add the water and stock powder or may combine the stock & then bring to a boil over high or maybe medium heat.
8. Please stir in the celery, oats, squash, Herbes de Provence & salt then return to a boil.
9. Reduce the heat to medium, cover & cook at gentle boil until squash is soft.
10. Approximately eighteen minutes.

11. Now puree the soup with your immersion blender or maybe cool slightly & then shift in small batches to a food process or maybe a blender and blend until smooth and creamy.
12. Whisk in enough vinegar to heighten the flavors.
13. One thing remains to be done now.
14. Now please adjust salt if needed, & then reheat if necessary.
15. Please garnish with chives.
16. Smell the aroma and serve.

Most subtle and definitive recipe!!

Yummy Chinese Spare Ribs with Garlic

This is the king recipe out there.

What you need

- 1 1/2 -2 tsp sea salt
- 2 - 3 tsp granular sugar
- 1/4cup garlic cloves, sliced or sliced
- One-Two tablespoon ginger pureed or maybe grated
- 1 1/2 -2 tablespoons reg. coconut aminos
- 1/2 cup minced green onion
- 1/ 1/2-2 Tbsps dry sherry
- 1-2 tbsp sesame oil

- 1-2 teaspoon ground black pepper
- 2.5 pounds pork spareribs in 1" 1/2" pieces
- 1 - 2 teaspoon chili garlic sauce

the method of preparation

1. Assemble all the ingredients at one place.
2. Blend entire of your ingredients in a large bowl. Now you should add your pork spareribs and mix well to cover.
3. Now please marinate for 1/2 hour at the room temperature.
4. Now we may proceed to the next most important step.

5. Now add about one cup of water to the pressure cooker & then now you should add your sparerib mixture.
6. One thing remains to be done now.
7. Now please bring the pressure cooker to high pressure and then cook for another eighteen minutes. After your cooking time allow your cooker to come to a natural release
8. Withdraw your spareribs from the cooker and garnish with the minced green onion and if you desire, cilantro leaves.

9. Smell the aroma & now you can serve.

The awesome smell used to fill my room as soon as used to uncover the plate.

Fantasy APPLESAUCE

It is very easy and quick recipe.

Ingredients:

- ¼ sugar
- About 12 Jonagold apples peeled cored and sliced
- ¼ cup water or maybe apple juice
- 1-2 tsp cinnamon

Instructions:

1. Please assemble all the ingredients at one place.
2. Please combine all of the ingredients to the pot of the pressure cooker and add.
3. Now we may proceed to the next step.

4. Lock lid input, set to HIGH and allow apples to cook for approximately 3 minutes once cooker has reached full pressure.
5. Use Quick Release method once apples are finished cooking.
6. One thing remains to be done now.
7. Stir mixture to break apart larger chunks and thoroughly combine within a consistent sauce. If you'd love a smoother consistency, utilize an immersion blender to break apart any remaining lumps.
8. Smell the aroma and serve.

Enjoy this fantastic recipe and eat it in one go.

King sized Apple Cider Breakfast Pulled Beef

It is excellent as well as super yummy.

Ingredients:

- 1-2 red onion, sliced
- Salt and pepper to taste
- One cup apple cider vinegar
- One thyme sprig
- Two-three pounds beef roast
- One rosemary sprig
- One-Two garlic cloves, crushed
- One apple peeled and diced

The method of preparation:

1. Assemble all the ingredients at one place.
2. Combine entire the ingredients in your pressure cooker.
3. One thing remains to be done now.
4. Now you should add salt and pepper to taste and cook on high pressure for 1 ½ hours.
5. When done, shred the beef within beautiful threads and now serve it warm in sandwiches.
6. Smell the aroma and now you can serve.

Perfect start of the day it is one of the rarest recipes

Speedy Chicken foresaw

Now why are you waiting? The supreme recipe is just below!! Learn it by heart.

What you need:

- Black pepper, 1 - 2 tsp
- Two sliced onion medium
- Cheddar cheese half cup
- Salsa for garnishing
- Two Diced tomatoes
- Green chilies 1-2 shredded
- 3 - 4tablespoons butter
- Whip cream half cup
- One cup chicken broth
- three-four garlic cloves
- Dried cumin 1-2 tbsp
- Garlic powder 2 - 3 tsp

- 1 pound of boneless chicken
- Sour cream 2-3 tablespoon

Method:

1. Assemble all the ingredients at one place.
2. Make cubes of chicken- approximately half an inch, One/Two in.
3. Add the dried ingredients to the chicken and blend well.
4. Now you should add rest of the ingredients.
5. Now we may proceed to the next most important step.
6. Transfer the ingredients to the pressure cooker.
7. Now you should add a tsp of oil to it.

8. Cover the cooker and switch the stove on for about four minutes.
9. Release the pressure by lifting the weights afterwards switching the stove off.
10. One thing remains to be done now.
11. Do not open the cover till all pressure gets released.
12. Take out the cooked meal and now you can serve by garnishing hot salsa.
13. Smell the aroma and serve.

Epic Lentil Breakfast Risotto

I always said that it was different, try it out!!

What you need:-

- 1 - 2 cloves of garlic, lightly mashed
- 1/2 - 1 tablespoon. of olive oil
- 3¼ cups of vegetable stock
- One medium onion, shredded
- One cup of dry lentils, soak in water for overnight
- One cup of Arborio rice
- One stalk of celery, chopped
- Parsley to taste

Directions:-

1. Assemble all the ingredients at one place.
2. In a pre-heated pressure cooker, add onion, parsley, celery rice and garlic together. Blend well.
3. Combine lentils and vegetable stock in the pot.
4. Now we may proceed to the next most important step.
5. Close and lock cooker's lid and cook for eight minutes at high setting.
6. One thing remains to be done now.
7. Now when the time is up, please open the pressure cooker by naturally releasing the pressure.

8. Now serve with a swirl of extra-virgin olive oil.
9. Smell the aroma and serve.

I used to go to my neighbor's house to eat this one.

Cooking time: 22 minutes

Servings: 5 -6

Delicious Pork Chops and Cabbage in Mushroom Sauce

What you need

- 3/4 cup low sodium pure chicken stock
- 1-2 teaspoon unrefined sea salt
- 1 cup sliced mushroom
- 1 (1lb) small head of cabbage
- 4 (3/four in) thick cut lean pork chops
- 1 - 2 tablespoon extra virgin olive oil
- 1-2 teaspoon ground black pepper
- 2 - 3 tsp almond flour

Directions

1. Assemble all the ingredients at one place.
2. Season your pork chops using the salt and pepper.
3. Slice the cabbage in half and then slice each half into 3/4 inch pieces setting them away.
4. Now we may proceed to the next most important step.
5. Now using the olive oil, grease the bottom of your pressure cooker and without putting the lid on your cooker place it on medium-high heat. Once your cooker is heated add the pork chops and brown them on one side, once

browned on one side, move them to a plate and set apart for the moment.

6. Toss the cabbage into the pressure cooker and arrange the pork chops brown side up above the cabbage. Now pour the chicken stock around the edges.

7. One thing remains to be done now.

8. Close and lock the lid of the pressure cooker and bring to a pressure over high heat and then you should lower the heat to the minimum required by the cooker to maintain pressure.

9. Cook for six-eight minutes at high pressure. Release the pressure.
10. Smell the aroma and serve.

Mystical CARROT CAKE OATS

Carrots are highly nutritious and when it is tasty, cloud nine!!

Ingredients:

- ¼- 1 teaspoon salt
- 1 cup steel now cut oats
- ¼ cup chia seeds
- One cup grated carrots
- 2-3 tbsps. maple syrup
- 1-2 tbsp. butter
- 2 - 3 tsp cinnamon
- 1 - 2 teaspoon pumpkin pie spice
- 4 cups water
- ¾ cup raisins

The method of preparation:

1. Assemble all the ingredients at one place.
2. Begin by adding butter to the pressure cooker and selecting SAUTE.
3. Now we may proceed to the next most important step.
4. Once the butter has totally melted, add oats and stir for about 4 minutes.
Afterwards adding, spices, carrots, water, salt and syrup, set cooker to HIGH and now allow for oats to cook for an additional 13 minutes.
5. Once cooking has completed, use Natural Release and now allow

mixture to cool for approximately 12 minutes.
6. One thing remains to be done now.
7. Use a Quick Pressure Release to alleviate any additional pressure before removing the cooker's lid.
8. After giving the oats a stir, blend in raisins and chia seeds. Cover oatmeal and now allow to sit for 5 to 10 minutes or until oats have reached proper thickness.
9. Smell the aroma and serve.

Now why are you waiting? The supreme recipe is just below!! Learn it by heart.

Super Breakfast Red Beans with Sausages

Red beans alongwith sausages are lovely and can be used to fill in.

Ingredients:

- One thyme sprig
- One can be red beans, drained
- Salt and pepper to taste
- One cup diced tomatoes
- ½-1 cup water
- 1 - 2 chorizo links, sliced
- One bay leaf
- 1 red onion, sliced
- ¼- 1 teaspoon Cajun seasoning
- 1 garlic clove, chopped

The method of preparation:

1. Assemble all the ingredients at one place.
2. Mix all the ingredients in your pressure cooker.
3. One thing remains to be done now.
4. Combine salt and pepper to taste and cooking on high pressure for twelve minutes.
5. Now allow to cool down for twelve minutes then release the pressure, and now you can serve the dish warm and fresh.
6. Smell the aroma and serve.

Simple ones do the job!!

Supreme Garlic Bread

I've always loved them. Plus they can be eaten anytime!!

Ingredients:

- 3 - 4 tablespoons butter
- 2 - 3 teaspoon baking powder
- Water, 2 cups
- 6-8 ounces cream cheese
- 1 cup blanched almond flour
- 1 - 2 teaspoon salt
- 1 - 2 large eggs

Method:

1. Assemble all the ingredients at one place.
2. Blend entire of the ingredients.

3. Now you should add the mixture to the bread baking pan.
4. Combine water within the pressure cooker.
5. Place the tray inside.
6. Now we may proceed to the next most important step.
7. Cover the cooker and switch the stove on for approximately twelve minutes.
8. Release the pressure by lifting the weights afterwards switching the stove off.
9. One thing remains to be done now.
10. Do not open the cover till all pressure is released.

11. Now serve and enjoy.
12. Smell the aroma and now serve.

Legendary Oatmeal with Caramelized apples

This is the one recipe you should look for.

Ingredients:-

- Apple pieces to taste
- 1/2 teaspoon sugar
- 1 - 2 teaspoon of butter
- ¾ cup of milk
- ¾ cup of cold water
- ½ cup of old fashioned oats
- 1-2 tbsp butter
- 1/4- 1/2 teaspoon coarse kosher salt
- 1/2- 1 tsp of brown sugar
- 1-2 tablespoon. desired Maple Syrup

Instructions:-

1. Assemble all the ingredients at one place.
2. Now you should add oats and ¼ teaspoon kosher salt and ¼ tsp sugar to the pressure cooker.
3. Combine ¾ cup of water, ¾ cup of milk and one tablespoon of butter. Cook at high pressure over high heatenup for six minutes. When time is up, remove from heatenup and release the pressure with quick pressure release method.
4. Now we may proceed to the next most important step.
5. Wash and Slice desired amount of apple for topping.

6. Heat apple pieces in the skillet on low-medium fire. Cooking till apple slice becomes soft.
7. Now you should add 1/2 tsp of butter, Two tbsp. of maple syrup
8. Once apples become soft, add 1 teaspoon of brown sugar and increase the heat to medium-high. Cook and Stirring frequently, till apple slices become dark golden colour.
9. When time is up, naturally release the pressure for 15 minutes, then use quick pressure release method release the remaining

pressure. Carefully unlock the lid and remove it.

10. One thing remains to be done now.
11. Transfer oatmeal within a serving bowl, whisk.
12. Combine caramelized apple slices on top of oatmeal, and now you can serve before it gets cold.
13. Smell the aroma & now you can serve.

Cooking time: twenty-three minutes approx

Serves: 1 - 2

Extraordinary Cook BAKED BANANAS

What you need:

- Two-three teaspoon salt
- 1 - 2 teaspoon baking soda
- Half cup sugar
- Nine bananas, under ripe and peeled
- ½ cup water
- 1 cup butter

The method of preparation:

1. Assemble all the ingredients at one place.
2. Add butter, soda, sugar, water, and salt into the pressure cooker.
3. Slice bananas into large pieces and add to mixture.

4. Bring pressure cooker to full heat, and once the temperature has peaked, set pressure to LOW.
5. Now we may proceed to the next most important step.
6. Now allow bananas to cook for twelve minutes, shaking the cooker every 5 minutes.
7. Use the Natural Release method to regulate pressure and withdraw cooker from heat.
8. Once pressure cooker has depressurized, use a spoon to toss banana pieces.
9. One thing remains to be done now.
10. Now please bring the cooker back to full pressure

& please cook bananas for an additional 15 minutes.
11. Afterwards cooking time is up, now allow the pressure cooker to depressurize and now allow for bananas to cool.
12. Smell the aroma & now you can serve.

Awesome Crustless Bacon Quiche

Not hard on your pocket so cheers!! It is excellent as well as super delightful.

What you need:

- One green onion, chopped
- One cup grated Cheddar cheese
- Salt and pepper to taste
- 5-6 bacon slices, chopped
- 5-6 eggs, beaten
- ½-One cup canned sweet corn, drained
- ¼ cup whole milk
- One-Two Chorizo sausage links, sliced

Instructions:

1. Assemble all the ingredients at one place.
2. Now pour about 1 cup of water at the bottom of the pot & place a metal trivet on sprinkle.
3. Prepare a small baking pan that fits the pressure cooker.
4. Now we may proceed to the next most important step.
5. Blend the eggs, Chorizo, green onion, milk, corn, bacon, salt and pepper in a bowl.
6. Pour the mixture into the prepared pan and sprinkle with cheese.
7. Cook on high pressure for 32 minutes.

8. When done, turn the pot off and allow to cool down for 12 minutes then release the pressure.
9. One thing remains to be done now.
10. Open the lid and shift the quiche on your board.
11. Now you can serve it warm or chilled.
12. Smell the aroma and serve.

Fantasy Lamb roasts with herb sauce

Not hard on your pocket so cheers!! It is very easy and quick recipe.

Ingredients:

- 1/2 half cup of whip cream
- 1/2 cup of virgin olive oil
- Hot sauce, 1-2 tsp
- Lamb meat cubes, One- 1/2 pounds
- Capsicum One cup
- 1/2-One half cup lamb broth
- 4- 5 tbsp of butter
- 1 cup cheered cheese
- Onion Two chopped
- 1 - 2 teaspoon of salt or as desired

- Black pepper 1-2 tsp or maybe as desired
- Four-five large cloves of garlic
- Vinegar 2 - 3 tbsp

Method:

1. Assemble all the ingredients at one place.
2. Grab a pan and add entire of the vegetables onto a skillet, ready to be fried with the olive oil, and put the stove on medium heat, stir continuously till the washed lamb meat and vegetables are cooked.
3. Use a deep pan and shift all of the ingredients to it.

4. Now you should add everything except for the lamb broth, mix well.
5. Now we may proceed to the next most important step.
6. Now you should add the entire mixture directly to the cooker.
7. Now you should add broth.
8. Cover the cooker & switch the stove on for about 22 minutes.
9. Release the pressure by lifting the weights after switching the stove off.
10. One thing remains to be done now.
11. Do not open the cover until entire of the pressure gets released.

12. Place the meal onto a serving platter, garnish with coriander leaves or maybe basil leaves (optional), and now serve.
13. Smell the aroma and serve.
14. This is the one recipe you should probably look for.

Great and simple recipe!!

Mystical EINKORN & YOGURT

Mystical, ummm, maybe. Depends on your opinion☺

What you need:

- ¼-1 teaspoon ginger
- ½ cup plain whole milk yogurt
- ¼-1 teaspoon cloves
- Fruits
- 1 - 2 tbsp honey
- Half cup einkorn wheat berries
- 1 - 2 tbsp Brown sugar
- ¼- 1 tsp nutmeg
- ¼ cup nuts of choice

Instructions:

1. Assemble all the ingredients at one place.
2. Several hours in advance, soak einkorn in water if possible.
3. Use two: One liquid to wheat berry while soaking.
4. When ready to cook, drain einkorn and water to pressure cooker set to HIGH.
5. Now we can proceed to the subsequent most important step.
6. Cooking for twelve minutes once cooker has attained pressure.
7. Once einkorn has finished cooking,

8. Utilize the Natural Release method and allow einkorn to depressurize.
9. One thing remains to be done now.
10. Serve with yogurt (or maybe milk), add fruits or maybe nuts if desired.
11. For combined sweetener, mix in brown sugar and hOney to cooked wheat berries.
12. Smell the aroma and serve.

Yoghurt makes it awesome!!

Awesome Ham Egg Muffins

Muffins!!

Ingredients:

- 1/2- 1 cup diced ham
- One cup grated Cheddar
- One green onion, sliced
- One/Two-1 red bell pepper, cored and diced
- five-6 eggs, beaten
- 1 garlic clove, chopped
- 1 - 2 tablespoons chopped parsley
- Salt and pepper to taste

Directions:

1. Assemble entire the ingredients at one place.
2. Blend the eggs, parsley, onion, bell pepper, garlic,

ham, salt and pepper in a bowl.
3. Now pour 1 cup of water in your pressure cooker. Arrange a steaming basket on sprinkle.
4. Now we may proceed to the next most important step.
5. Now pour the egg mixture into seven muffin cups and put them all on a sprinkle of the steaming basket.
6. Cover every muffin with grated cheese then seal the pot with its lid.
7. One thing remains to be done now.
8. Cook on high pressure for 5 minutes.

9. Now serve the muffins warm, only afterwards you've carefully released the pressure of the pot.
10. Smell the aroma and now you can serve.

With Ham, it certainly deserves a try!!

Fantastic Pressure cooker fruity beef stew

It is excellent as well as super delightful.

What you need:

- Onion 2 sliced
- Raspberries quarter cup
- Pineapple chunks half cup
- Coconut oil 3 – 4 tablespoon
- Almond oil Two-three tablespoon
- Cubed 1/2 pound of beef
- Garlic powder One-Two teaspoon
- Baby carrots half cup
- Vinegar 2 - 3 tsp
- Soy sauce 1 - 2 teaspoon

Method:

1. Assemble all the ingredients at one place.
2. Take a bowl and add meat in it.
3. Now you should add rest of the ingredients.
4. Marinate meat with entire the ingredients except both types of oil.
5. Now we may proceed to the next most important step.
6. Now you should add oil at the end.
7. Spare few oil to be added to the pressure cooker.
8. Switch on the stove and combine oil to the cooker.
9. Shift the beef materials to the pressure cooker.

10. Cover the cooker & then switch the stove on for approximately 18 minutes or so.
11. Release the pressure by lifting the weights, afterwards switching the stove off.
12. One thing remains to be done now.
13. Do not open the cover until the entire pressure gets released.
14. Take out the cooked meal and now you can serve.

Enjoy this fantastic recipe & eat it in one go.

Legendary ITALIAN OMELETTE

The wonderful smell used to fill my room as soon as used to uncover the plate.

What you need:

- 1-2 cups mozzarella cheese
- 1 (12 oz.) box frozen spinach
- Two-three eggs
- Two or 3 cook or Baked potatoes
- 1 cup milk
- Seasoning salt
- Parmesan cheese
- 2-3 tbsp mayonnaise
- Cayenne pepper

The method of preparation:

1. Assemble all the ingredients at one place.
2. Oil pressure cooker pot liberally and set to HIGH.
3. Now cut potatoes into thin slices and top with seasoning salt and parmesan cheese; Layer bottom of the pan with potato pieces.
4. Thaw out spinach in the microwave with a few teaspoons of water.
5. Now we may proceed to the next most important step.
6. Drain spinach once it is unfrozen and proceed to press out residual water with a spatula.

7. In a distinct bowl, mix onion powder, garlic, cheese and mayonnaise along with a bit of cayenne pepper if desired.
8. Now, spread mayonnaise mixture on top of potatoes. Add spinach on top of mayonnaise.
9. One thing remains to be done now.
10. In another bowl, crush together eggs, milk, salt and pepper and pour on a sprinkle of potatoes and spinach.
11. Top with additional cheese.
12. Shut the lid & then cook for about 4 minutes;

When cook time is up, use the Quick Release method to bring the pressure back to normal.
13. Smell the aroma and serve.

Forgotten LADI PAV

Sizzle your taste buds and get the taste of this simple yet tantalizing recipe.

Ingredients:

- 2½ cups whole wheat flour
- One-Two teaspoon salt
- One-Two teaspoon sugar
- 1 1/2- 2 tsp yeast
- Half cup entire-purpose flour
- 1 cup warm water
- One-Two tbsp oil

How to prepare:

1. Assemble all the ingredients at one place.

2. Blend together yeast, warm water, sugar, and stirring to combine.
3. Now you should add flour and continue to stir until batter-love consistency is attained.
4. Cover flour mixture and set away for approximately 32 minutes, or until mixture has doubled in size.
5. Now we may proceed to the next most important step.
6. Once the dough has risen, work dough within a loaf and slice into equal pieces.
7. Roll slices into individual balls and put in a greased pan, being sure to leave

space in between every ball.
8. Cover once more and allow the dough to rise for an additional 12 minutes.
9. In pressure cooker pot, add One cup of salt to the bottom of the pot, creating an even layer of salt. Heat on LOW for approximately 6 minutes before adding the baking pan with dough to cooker.
10. One thing remains to be done now.
11. Secure lid and continue to cook on LOW for approximately 30 minutes.

12. Afterwards, cook time is up, depressurize cooker and remove pan.
13. Transfer to wire rack; Once cooled off, now you can serve with oil or maybe butter.
14. Smell the aroma and serve.

Lovely Mediterranean Artichoke Breakfast Casserole

I've been wondering about this recipe, so I decided to include it in my collection.

What you need:

- ½ -1 tsp dried oregano
- 3- 4 artichoke hearts, shredded
- ¼ cup milk
- Salt and pepper to taste
- One green onion, shredded
- 1 cup baby spinach
- 5- 6 eggs, beaten
- half-1 teaspoon dried basil
- One red bell pepper, cored and diced
- 3-4 sun-dried tomatoes, sliced

- Two-three tablespoons grated Parmesan

The method of preparation:

1. Assemble entire the ingredients at one place.
2. Mix entire the ingredients in a bowl and season with salt and pepper.
3. Grease a small deep dish baking pan with butter or maybe oil. Make sure the pan can fit the pressure cooker.
4. Now we may proceed to the next most important step.
5. Now pour one cup of water in your pressure cooker then arrange a metal trivet on sprinkle.

6. Now, pour the egg mixture into the prepared pan and then put the pan over the metal trivet.
7. One thing remains to be done now.
8. Seal the pan with its lid and cook on high pressure for 15 minutes.
9. Now serve the casserole warm and fresh.
10. Smell the aroma and serve.

I bet that you'll love it.

Amazing Sweet Meatloaf

Just try it if you want.

Ingredients:

- Onion One chopped
- Strawberries half cup
- Pineapple chunks 1 cup
- Blueberries half cup
- Olive oil 1 - 2 tsp
- Garlic powder 1 - 2 tsp
- Beef cutlets 1/2 pound
- Ginger 2 - 3 tablespoons
- Coconut milk 3-4 tablespoons
- Soy sauce 1-2 teaspoon
- Almond oil 2-3 tbsp

Method:

1. Assemble all the ingredients at one place.

2. Take a bowl and now you should add meat cutlets into it.
3. Combine entire of the ingredients to it, one by one.
4. Do not now you should add oil initially, but combine it afterwards making the mixture smooth and consistent.
5. Now we may proceed to the next most important step.
6. Spare some oil to be added to the pressure cooker.
7. Switch on the stove and now you should add oil and water to the cooker.
8. Cover the cooker for approximately 15 minutes.

9. Release the pressure by lifting weights and do not open the cooker till all the pressure gets released.
10. One thing remains to be done now.
11. Take out the meal and now you can serve hot.
12. You can garnish this recipe with coriander leaves or maybe mint leaves, you decide.
13. Smell the aroma and serve.

Mega MEXICAN BREAKFAST BURRITO

Burrito and that too Mexican!!

What you need:

- 1-2 teaspoon salt
- Six-eight eggs
- 1 avocado
- ½ cup tomato
- ¼ cup cilantro
- 1 - 2 tbsps. of olive oil
- ¼ cup water
- ¼ cup red onion
- Four gordita tortillas
- One cup black beans

Directions:

1. Assemble all the ingredients at one place.

2. Now, over medium heat, warm up olive oil in pressure cooker.
3. Now you should add eggs and sauté for several minutes before adding tomato, onion, cilantro, water, and salt.
4. Now we may proceed to the next most important step.
5. Lock lid and set pressure to high. Cooking for approximately 4 minutes or so.
6. Meanwhile, heat tortillas in microwave or on the stovetop. When eggs have finished cooking, power off the cooker and utilize the quick Release method.

7. Divide eggs evenly between tortillas.
8. Drain black beans and disperse evenly among tortillas.
9. One thing remains to be done now.
10. Slice avocado and now you should add to burritos.
11. Fold up burritos, being sure not to let stuffing spill out.
12. Smell the aroma and serve.

Tasty Soy Bean Chickpea Paste
You may never know how good it can be until you try out.

Ingredients:

- Salt and pepper to taste
- 1/2- 1 onion, shredded
- 12 oz. dried chickpeas
- four-six cups water
- Three-Four oz. soybeans
- 1 bay leaf
- One lemon juiced
- ½- 1 cup olive oil

Directions:

1. Assemble all the ingredients at one place.
2. Blend the soy beans, chickpeas, water, bay leaf

and onion in your pressure cooker.
3. Cover the pot and cook on high pressure for 1 ¼ hours.
4. Now we may proceed to the next most important step.
5. When done, release the pressure carefully and shift the beans in your pressure cooker.
6. One thing remains to be done now.
7. Now you should add the lemon juice and olive oil, as well as salt and pepper and pulse until smooth and creamy.
8. Now you can serve the paste fresh.
9. Smell the aroma and serve.

Fast OUEF EN COCOTTE

It is very easy and quick recipe.

What you need:

- Three-four slices of cheese or dash of heavy cream
- Olive oil
- Three-4 eggs
- 3 - 4pieces of meat, fish or veggies
- Fresh herbs

Instructions:

1. Assemble all the ingredients at one place.
2. Combine One cup of water to pressure cooker and set apart.

3. Now prepare four ramekins by coating the inside with olive oil.
4. Now we may proceed to the succeeding most important step.
5. Wrap meat vegetable slices inside of the ramekin and then crack an egg on a sprinkle of each bowl.
6. Sprinkle with cream, cheese, or maybe sprigs of herb such as basil.
7. One thing remains to be done now.
8. For soft eggs, tightly cover ramekin with aluminum foil before placing ramekin in a steamer basket.

9. Lower into pressure cooking and lock lid. Set heat to LOW and allow four minutes – afterwards, use Natural Release method to regulate pressure.
10. Smell the aroma and serve.

Fastest one!!

King-sized Sweet Potato Bread Pudding

Ever wondered what makes the cooks prepare such delicious food? Well, the answer is the excellent recipe they employ...

Ingredients:

- One cup rolled oats
- 6- 8 slices bread cubed
- 1/2-One pinch salt
- 3-4 eggs, beaten
- ¼ cup maple syrup
- 1 - 2 sweet potatoes, peeled and cubed
- One-Two teaspoon vanilla extract
- Two cups milk
- ½ cup dried cranberries
- Half cup golden raisins

How to prepare:

1. Assemble all the ingredients at one place.
2. Add all the ingredients in a bowl.
3. Grease a deep dish baking pan that fits your pressure cooker with butter or maybe oil. Pour the pudding mixture into the pan.
4. Now we may proceed to the next most important step.
5. Now pour one cup of water in your pressure cooker. Place a metal trivet on top then arrange the pan above the trivet.
6. One thing remains to be done now.

7. Cover the pot with its lid & then cook on high pressure for 22 minutes.
8. Allow it to cool down for twelve minutes then done then release the pressure and now you can serve the pudding chilled.
9. Smell the aroma and serve.

Cute POTATO BACON HASH BROWN

Potato Bacon!! Secret tip: Spice up the potatoes as much as you consider reasonable for an awesome taste.

Ingredients:

- 6-8 oz. bacon
- Salt and pepper to taste
- 1 - 2 tbsp. parsley
- 2 large russet potatoes
- 1 - 2 tbsp olive oil

How to prepare:

1. Assemble all the ingredients at one place.
2. Above medium heat, pour olive oil into the pressure cooker.

3. Now you should add potatoes, peeled, washed, and diced to the oil; Season with black pepper and salt to taste.
4. Now we may proceed to the next most important step.
5. Whisk occasionally until potatoes begin to brown.
6. Once the potatoes have finished cooking, combine cooked and crumbled bacon and parsley and mix well.
7. One thing remains to be done now.
8. Press down the potato-bacon mixture with a wide spatula and lock lid in place.

9. Cook on LOW for about 4 minutes before removing from heat and utilizing Quick Release method.
10. Smell the aroma and serve.

Historic SAUSAGE, PEPPERS, and ONIONS

Historic, yeah it is kind of old one!!

What you need:

- One-Two teaspoon garlic powder
- Three-four large green bell peppers, sliced
- 1 - 2 tbsp. Italian seasoning
- One can tomato sauce
- One cup water
- Twelve sausages
- 1 - 2 tablespoon. basil
- One can dice tomatoes

How to prepare:

1. Assemble all the ingredients at one place.

2. Blend tomatoes, basil, garlic, sauce, water, and Italian seasoning and pour within pressure cooker pot.
3. Now we may proceed to the next most important step.
4. Add sausages and peppers without mixing the sauce.
5. One thing remains to be done now.
6. Secure lid input and set to HIGH and cook for approximately twenty-Two minutes.
7. Power off pressure cooker and use Quick Release to regulate pressure; serve once sausages have depressurized.
8. Smell the aroma and serve.

Printed in Great Britain
by Amazon